What Is the Moon Made Of?

And Other Questions Kids Have About Space

by Donna H. Bowman   illustrated by Peter Lubach

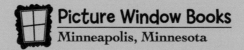

Picture Window Books
Minneapolis, Minnesota

Acknowledgments
This book was produced for Picture Window Books
by Bender Richardson White, U.K.

Illustrations by Peter Lubach
Consultant: Dr. Karl Gebhardt, Professor of Astronomy,
University of Texas

Picture Window Books
1710 Roe Crest Drive
North Mankato, MN 56003
877-845-8392
www.capstonepub.com

Library of Congress Cataloging-in-Publication Data
Bowman, Donna H.
What is the moon made of? : and other questions kids have about
space / by Donna H. Bowman ; illustrated by Peter Lubach.
p. cm. — (Kids' questions)
Includes index.
ISBN 978-1-4048-5529-8 (library binding)
ISBN 978-1-4048-6726-0 (paperback)
1. Moon—Juvenile literature. 2. Planets—Juvenile literature.
3. Solar system—Juvenile literature. 4. Outer space—Juvenile
literature. I. Lubach, Peter, ill. II. Title.
QB582.B69 2010
520—dc22   2009013099

SPACE

Kids have lots of questions about space. What is the moon made of? Is the sun a star? Why does space have no air? Has anyone been on Mars? In this book, kids' questions get answered.

How many planets are in space?

Dawson, age 8

There are eight planets in our solar system. All of them orbit, or circle, the sun. In order from the sun they are: Mercury, Venus, Earth, Mars, Jupiter, Saturn, Uranus, and Neptune.

SUN

NEPTUNE

Is there going to be a new planet?

1st and 2nd graders

Yes. New stars are forming in space all the time. When new stars form, so do planets. More than 300 new planets have been found outside our solar system. Telescopes help us find new stars and planets deep in space.

Why is Pluto called a dwarf planet?

Madison, age 8

What is Pluto made out of?

Jasen, age 7

Pluto is called a "dwarf" planet because it's very small. It is only 1,243 miles (1,989 kilometers) across. That's about twice the size of Texas. Pluto is made of water, ice, and rocks.

Why is Mars red?

Paul, age 8

Why do the planets look colored?

1st and 2nd graders

Mars looks red because of rust in the planet's soil. Venus looks bright orange because of volcanoes that throw gas into the air. Methane gas makes Neptune look blue.

5

Why does Earth spin around in circles?

1st and 2nd graders

Planets form in large clouds of energy. This energy makes the planets spin, or rotate. Once they start to spin, there is nothing to stop them. So they keep spinning. All planets, including Earth, rotate.

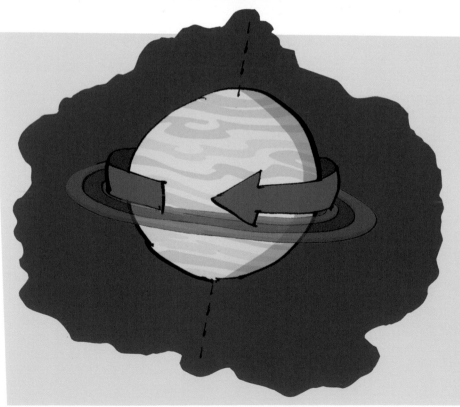

Does Saturn turn left or right?

Mia, age 8

Mercury, Earth, Mars, Jupiter, Saturn, and Neptune rotate to the right, or clockwise. Venus and Uranus rotate to the left, or counterclockwise.

How many rings does Saturn have?
Kindergartners

Can all the planets fit inside Saturn?
Corbin, age 8

What is the biggest planet?
Josie, age 8

Saturn has three main rings and thousands of smaller ones. Rings are made of dust, rock, and ice. Some of the ice chunks are the size of a house! Jupiter, Uranus, and Neptune also have rings.

Saturn's not big enough to hold the other seven planets. But Jupiter is! Jupiter is the biggest planet. Saturn is the lightest planet. If all the planets could fit in a huge pool of water, only Saturn would float.

SATURN'S RINGS

Which is the coldest planet?
Luis, age 8

Is Jupiter hot?
Jordan, age 6

Neptune is the coldest planet. Its temperature is minus 328 degrees Fahrenheit (minus 200 degrees Celsius). Jupiter's cold, too. It measures minus 166 degrees Fahrenheit (minus 110 degrees C).

The hottest planet is Venus. It is almost 900 degrees Fahrenheit (482 degrees C). Home ovens usually reach only 550 degrees Fahrenheit (288 degrees C).

NEPTUNE

VENUS

Is the sun really a star?
Paul, age 8

How many stars are in space?
Chloe, age 7

Yes, the sun is a star. It's one of many, many stars in the universe. About 100 billion galaxies in space each have around 100 billion stars. That's about 10 sextillion stars total—about as many grains of sand as are on Earth!

What is the sun made of?

Jasen, age 7

When will the sun explode?

Hollister, age 7

The sun is a giant ball of burning gases. It gives off a lot of heat and light. Scientists don't think it will ever explode. In billions of years, when the sun runs out of fuel, it will probably shrink into a small, weak star.

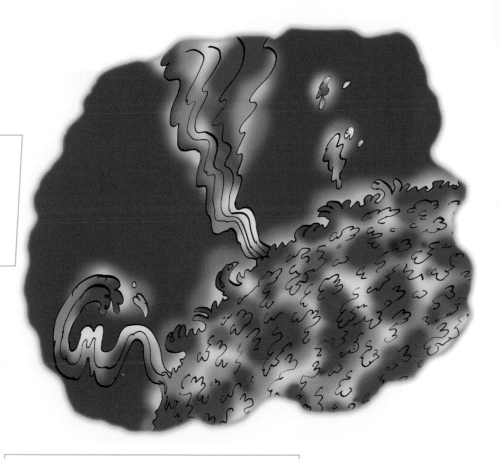

How hot is the sun?

Bereket, age 6

How many miles is the sun from Earth?

Niko, age 8

The sun's surface is about 10,832 degrees Fahrenheit (6,000 degrees C). The sun is nearly 93 million miles (149 million km) away. It is close enough to light and warm Earth. But it is far away enough not to boil our lakes, rivers, and oceans!

9

Where does the moon go when it disappears?

2nd graders

Are the sun and moon up at the same time in the early morning?

Cory Elementary School

How big is the moon?

Jole, age 7

How far is it to the moon?

Sarah, age 8

The moon disappears from view as it orbits behind Earth. We see only the part of the moon lit by the sun—often only a sliver. Sometimes the moon and sun rise and set together, but not often.

The moon is 6,835 miles (11,000 km) around its middle. To walk that far would take more than 140 days! The moon is 238,857 miles (382,171 km) from Earth. If a jet plane could fly to the moon, the journey would take about 17 days.

What is the moon made out of?
Jasen, age 7

How many craters are on the moon?
Jole, age 7

The moon is covered with lava rocks and 1.5 million craters (large and small pits). It is also covered with a 5- to 20-foot (1.5- to 6.1-meter) layer of gray soil.

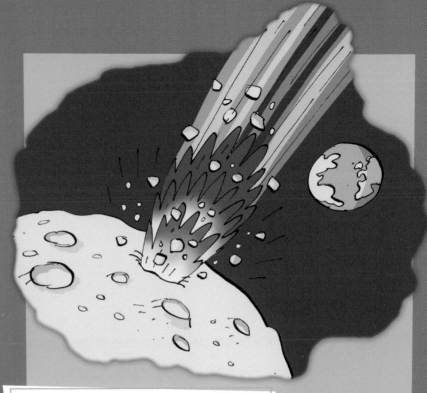

Are there rocks on the moon?
Sara, age 6

Why does the moon have a lot of bumps?
Justin, age 8

Yes, there are rocks on the moon. Meteorites hit the moon, blasting pits and scattering rocks. Unlike Earth, the moon has no volcanoes or earthquakes to reshape its surface. It also has no atmosphere (air) to slow down or burn up meteors before they hit the surface.

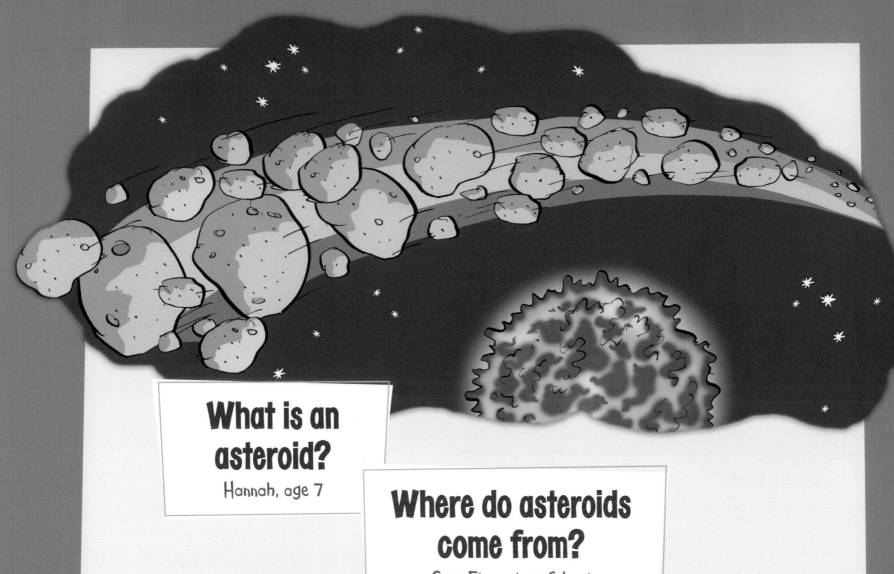

What is an asteroid?

Hannah, age 7

Where do asteroids come from?

Cory Elementary School

Asteroids are pieces of rock or metal that orbit the sun. They come in different sizes, shapes, and colors. Most asteroids in our solar system are found in the asteroid belt. The belt lies between Mars and Jupiter.

Planets formed in our solar system when pieces of space rock stuck to each other. But some pieces were unable to stick together. They became asteroids.

Why are asteroids in the asteroid belt stuck between Mars and Jupiter?

Alexandria Elementary School

Mars and Jupiter both tug on the asteroid belt. Neither planet's gravity is strong enough to pull the asteroids into its own orbit. The asteroids remain stuck in the middle.

Has anything from space ever hit a person on Earth?

Alexandria Elementary School

Yes, but it's rare. Throughout history, only 14 people have reported being hit by meteorites. In 1954, Ann Elizabeth Hodges of Alabama was struck by a 9-pound (4-kilogram) meteorite that smashed through the roof of her home. She was bruised, but she survived.

Why is it dark in space?

Kindergartners

Why does space stay black, but our sky gets bright during the day?

Sophia, age 8

We see light when it bounces off objects. Bright light bounces off tiny particles in Earth's atmosphere. Space has no atmosphere or particles, so most light in space remains unseen.

Why is there no gravity in space?

Chloe, age 7

Space has gravity everywhere, but in different amounts. The sun's strong gravity holds our solar system together. Gravity keeps all of us on Earth. Even the moon has some gravity. Without gravity, astronauts wouldn't be able to walk on the moon. They'd pop right off!

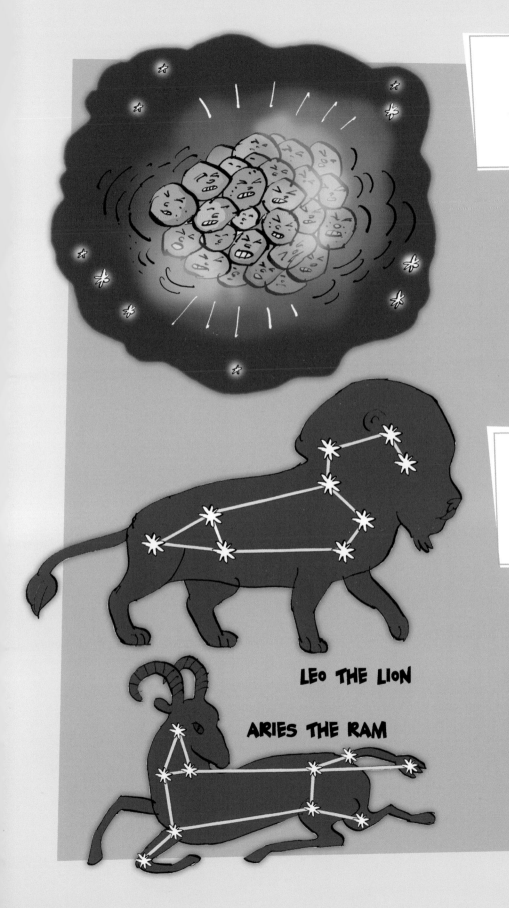

How are
stars made?
Javier, age 8

Stars form when gravity squishes together gas and dust in space. Gravity never pushes. It pulls everything toward it.

LEO THE LION

ARIES THE RAM

How many constellations
are there?
Haley, age 8

The sky is sorted into 88 groups of star pictures called constellations. Connecting the dots in the sky makes pictures of lions, rams, and more. The stars stay in the same pattern while moving across the sky.

What is the Milky Way?

Michelle, age 6

The Milky Way is a galaxy. It contains about 100 billion stars, including our sun. Everything that orbits the sun (including the planets, moons, and asteroids) is a very tiny part of the Milky Way galaxy.

How many galaxies are in space?

Chloe, age 7

In the space that we can see, there are about 100 billion galaxies. Galaxies, such as our Milky Way, are large spinning groups of stars, gas, rock, and dust. Galaxies vary in size and brightness.

Where are there black holes?

Cory Elementary School

Most galaxies likely have a black hole in their center. Black holes are made when giant stars crumble and die. Powerful gravity pulls in almost everything, including light.

Has anything come out of a black hole?

2nd graders

We don't know. Some scientists believe that nothing escapes black holes. Some believe black holes leak tiny bits of light and energy called "Hawking radiation." But these bits have not yet been seen.

17

Do aliens live in space?

Joe, age 8

Are there aliens on the planets?

Caren, age 5

No alien life has been found on other planets or anywhere else in space. But scientists keep looking! Life as we know it needs a planet with oxygen and water.

ATMOSPHERE AROUND EARTH

Why can't you breathe in space?

Ashley, age 6

Why does space have no air?

Caroline, age 8

Earth's atmosphere contains breathable gases, mostly nitrogen and oxygen. Other planets have poisonous mixes of gases. Gases are held in place by each planet's gravity. The space between planets has no gas, no atmosphere, nothing to breathe.

How long does space go on?
Amanda, age 7

Does space end?
Joe, age 8

How long does it take to get into space?
Madison, age 8

We're not sure how big space is. We see only a small part of it. It may go on forever, with no beginning and no end.

A spacecraft blasting off from Earth reaches space in about eight minutes. Space begins about 62 miles (99 km) above our planet.

Can you float even if you aren't on a spaceship?

Emily, age 7

How come you have to put helmets on in space?

Kailey, age 6

How come you have to wear a special suit?

Alex, age 6

Yes. Astronauts orbit Earth at about 17,500 miles (28,000 km) per hour, whether inside or outside the spacecraft. Nothing slows their speed. Astronauts aren't really floating, however. They're being pulled by gravity.

Inside a suit and helmet an astronaut stays comfortable and safe. Space is both much too cold and too hot for people. There is no oxygen to breathe, and the sun's rays are dangerously strong.

THE FIRST MOON FOOTPRINT

Where have people traveled in space?
Keara, age 7

How many people have been in space?
Brody, age 8

People have orbited Earth. They have also orbited and landed on the moon. More than 460 people from 34 countries have traveled into space. That number includes more than 400 men and 50 women.

How many astronauts have been on the moon?
Abigale, age 8

Between 1969 and 1972, 12 U.S. astronauts walked on the moon. Two astronauts at a time landed on the moon during the six Apollo missions.

Has anyone been on Mars?

Cory Elementary School

People have not yet visited Mars. The National Aeronautics and Space Administration (NASA) has sent remote-controlled machines to check it out. Information from these machines helps NASA plan for people to one day visit Mars.